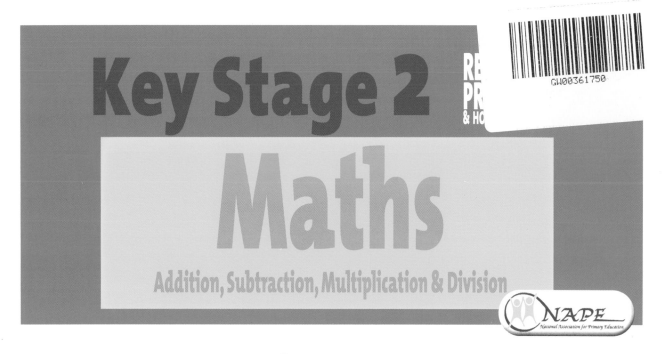

Key Stage 2

Maths

Addition, Subtraction, Multiplication & Division

Contents

AUTHOR: Camilla de la Bédoyère
EDITORIAL: John Cattermole, Vicky Garrard, Julia Rolf
DESIGN: Jen Bishop, Dave Jones
ILLUSTRATORS: Bridget Dowty, Sarah Wimperis
PRODUCTION: Chris Herbert, Claire Walker

COMMISSIONING EDITOR: Polly Willis
PUBLISHER AND CREATIVE DIRECTOR: Nick Wells

3 Book Pack ISBN 1-84451-087-5   Book ISBN 1-84451-042-5
6 Book Pack ISBN 1-84451-090-5   Book ISBN 1-84451-097-2

First published in 2004

A copy of the CIP data for this book is available from the British Library upon request.

Created and produced by
FLAME TREE PUBLISHING
Crabtree Hall,
Crabtree Lane,
Fulham, London SW6 6TY
United Kingdom
www.flametreepublishing.com

Flame Tree Publishing is part of The Foundry Creative Media Co. Ltd.

© The Foundry Creative Media Co. Ltd, 2004

Printed in Croatia

Foreword

Sometimes when I am crossing the playground on my way to visit a primary school I pass young children playing at schools. There is always a stern authoritarian little teacher at the front laying down the law to the unruly group of children in the pretend class. This puzzles me a little because the school I am visiting is very far from being like the children's play. Where do they get this Victorian view of what school is like? Perhaps it's handed down from generation to generation through the genes. Certainly they don't get it from their primary school. Teachers today are more often found alongside their pupils, who are learning by actually doing things for themselves, rather than merely listening and obeying instructions.

Busy children, interested and involved in their classroom reflect what we know about how they learn. Of course they learn from teachers but most of all they learn from their experience of life and their life is spent both in and out of school. Indeed, if we compare the impact upon children of even the finest schools and teachers, we find that three or four times as great an impact is made by the reality of children's lives outside the school. That reality has the parent at the all important centre. No adult can have so much impact, for good or ill, as the young child's mother or father.

This book, and others in the series, are founded on the sure belief that the great majority of parents want to help their children grow and learn and that teachers are keen to support them. The days when parents were kept at arm's length from schools are long gone and over the years we have moved well beyond the white line painted on the playground across which no parent must pass without an appointment. Now parents move freely in and out of schools and very often are found in the classrooms backing up the teachers. Both sides of the partnership know how important it is that children should be challenged and stimulated both in and out of school.

Perhaps the most vital part of this book is where parents and children are encouraged to develop activities beyond those offered on the page. The more the children explore and use the ideas and techniques we want them to learn, the more they will make new knowledge of their very own. It's not just getting the right answer, it's growing as a person through gaining skill in action and not only in books. The best way to learn is to live.

I remember reading a story to a group of nine year old boys. The story was about soldiers and of course the boys, bloodthirsty as ever, were hanging on my every word. I came to the word khaki and I asked the group "What colour is khaki?" One boy was quick to answer. "Silver" he said, "It's silver." "Silver? I queried. "Yes," he said with absolute confidence, "silver, my Dad's car key is silver." Now I reckon I'm a pretty good teller of stories to children but when it came down to it, all my dramatic reading of a gripping story gave way immediately to the power of the boy's experience of life. That meant so much more to him, as it does to all children.

JOHN COE
General Secretary, National Association for Primary Education (NAPE).

Parents and teachers work together in NAPE to improve the quality of learning and teaching in primary schools. We campaign hard for a better deal for children at the vital early stage of their education upon which later success depends. We are always pleased to hear from parents.

NAPE, Moulton College, Moulton, Northampton, NN3 7RR,
Telephone: 01604 647 646 Web: www.nape.org.uk

Addition, Subtraction, Multiplication & Division is one of six books in the **Revision, Practice & Home Learning** series, which has been devised to help you support your child as they revise for their SATs exams at the end of Year Six.

The National Curriculum gives teachers clear guidelines on what subjects should be studied in Mathematics, and to what level. These guidelines have been used to form the content of both this book and **Shape, Size & Distance**, the accompanying maths text in this series.

Each page contains revision notes, exercises for your child to complete, an activity they can complete away from the book (**Activity** boxes) and practical pointers to give you extra information and guidance (**Parents Start Here** boxes). At the end of the book you will find a checklist of topics – you can use this to mark off each topic as it is mastered.

This book has been designed for children to work through alone; but it is recommended that you read the book first to acquaint yourself with the material it contains. Try to be at hand when your child is working with the book; your input is valuable. The teaching of mathematics has changed since you were at school and you may find you can learn something useful too!

Encourage good study habits in your child:

- Try to set aside a short time every day for studying. Ten to 20 minutes a day is plenty. Establish a quiet and comfortable environment for your child to work

- Give your child access to drinking water whenever they work; research suggests this helps them perform better.

- Reward your child; plenty of praise for good work motivates children to succeed.

- Keep a maths kit to hand; this should contain pencils, ruler, paper, scissors, measuring tape, jar of counters, calculator, compass, protractor, squared paper and dice.

This book is intended to support your child in their school work. Sometimes children find particular topics hard to understand; discuss this with their teacher, who may be able to suggest alternative ways to help your child.

Top Tip! Remember to give your child lots of praise – they will work so much better.

Parents Start Here...

By the end of Year Six children should be able to write whole numbers in figures and words and use decimal notation for tenths and hundreds in calculations. They need to know what each number represents up to three decimal places.

Ordering Numbers

Remember!

- Every number can be written in both words and digits.

- Every digit in a number has a place value.

- Digits after a decimal point represent tenths, hundredths and thousandths.

1. Fill in this number square up to 10:

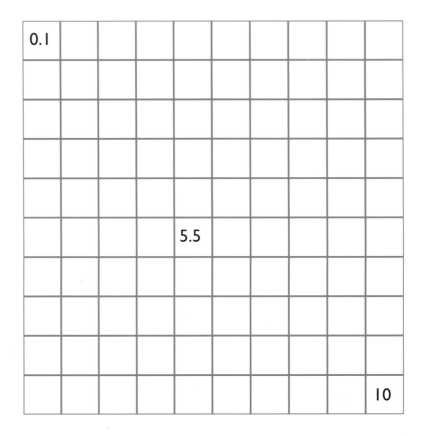

2. Write these numbers as words:

a) 340 _____

b) 1502 _____

c) 98 _____

3. Put these numbers in to the chart. The first one has been done for you:

	hundreds	tens	units	tenths	hundredths
346.3	300	40	6	3	0
45.03					
0.98					
904.56					
70.24					

4. a) What is the value of the digit 8 in 86 342? _____

b) What is the 4 worth in 8.74? _____

c) Write the number that is equivalent to 6 thousands, 3 hundreds,

2 tens and 3 units _____

Activity

Copy out a blank Number Square, like the one you completed on page 4. Start it with a different number, any number you like, and fill it in. Can you predict what the final number will be before you get there? Look for patterns.

Check Your Progress!
Ordering Numbers

Turn to page 48 and put a tick next to what you have just learned.

Top Tip! Go through any of the questions on these pages as often as you like until your child understands it fully.

Parents Start Here...

Use a metre rule with centimetres marked on. Point to any number on the rule and ask your child what the difference is between that number and 100. You can set similar puzzles to this using the meter rule (or a measuring tape).

Adding Up To 100

Remember!

- Two numbers that add up to 100 are number bonds.

- You need to know all of the number bonds up to 100.

- You can chop numbers up to add them. This is called partitioning.

1. Look at this sum:

$$24 + 65 =$$

Add up the tens first:	20 + 60 = 80
Then the units:	4 + 5 = 9
Then the totals:	80 + 9 = 89

Use this example to complete these sums. Write down each step:

a) 75 + 21 =

_____

_____

_____

b) 26 + 37 =

_____

_____

_____

c) 73 + 16 =

_____

_____

_____

d) 51 + 47 =

_____

_____

_____

2. Complete these sums the same way, but this time do the addition in your head:

a) 66 + 15 = _____

b) 40 + 29 = _____

c) 39 + 61 = _____

d) 55 + 43 = _____

3. Fill in the boxes:

a) 36 + ☐ = 100   b) 100 − ☐ = 36

c) 45 + ☐ = 100   d) 100 − 45 = ☐

4. Joseph has put 100 pencils in a box. 44 of them are red and the rest are blue. How many blue pencils are there?

_____

Activity

When you spend less than a pound in a shop try to work out, in your head, what the change would be from a pound coin.

Check Your Progress!
Adding Up To 100
Turn to page 48 and put a tick next to what you have just learned.

7

Top Tip! Try and incorporate what your child learns into everyday life – they will remember it even better.

Parents Start Here...

It is less confusing to your child if you say 'negative 3' rather than 'minus 3': children think of 'minus' meaning the same as 'subtract'.

Negative Numbers

Remember!

- Negative numbers are less than zero.

- You count negative numbers back from zero.

- Negative numbers can be added and subtracted just like numbers above zero.

- The best way to revise negative numbers is to use a number line.

1. Use these number lines to help you work out these additions and subtractions. You can write your own numbers in. Remember to bounce backwards when you subtract:

a)

-4 + 5 = ☐

b)

4 − 5 = ☐

8

c)

-20 + 8 =

d)

2 − 9 =

e)

-56 − 3 =

f)

-78 − 6 =

g)

-15 + 4 =

Activity

Negative numbers can be confusing. Try to think of them in terms of money or temperatures and then they make more sense. Play with a calculator and experiment with negative numbers.

Check Your Progress!
Negative Numbers
Turn to page 48 and put a tick next to what you have just learned.

Parents Start Here...

Ensure your child can manipulate decimals as described on these pages before they try adding and subtracting decimals using the Column Method.

Decimals

Remember!

- Decimals are numbers that have a decimal point.

- The decimal point separates the whole numbers from the numbers that are part of a whole number.

- When you do calculations it matters where you put the decimal points.

- When we write money calculations we use a decimal point to show the parts of a pound (pence).

- We can round up or down to a nearest whole number. If your number is halfway between two whole numbers always round up.

- We use the symbol ≈ to show 'approximately'.

1. Write each decimal number and write which whole number it is closest to. The first one has been done for you:

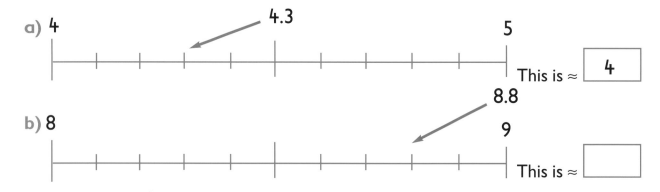

a) 4   4.3   5   This is ≈ 4

b) 8   8.8   9   This is ≈

c) 2   2.4   3   This is ≈ ☐

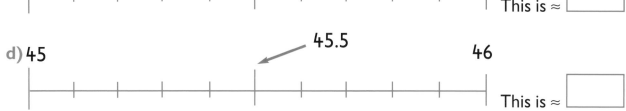

d) 45   45.5   46   This is ≈ ☐

2. Write each decimal to the nearest whole number:

a) 6.7 ≈ ☐   b) 59.9 ≈ ☐

c) £3.40 ≈ ☐   d) £78.90 ≈ ☐

3. Write the missing numbers:

a) 4.1 + ☐ = 5.0   b) 2.3 + ☐ = 3

c) £7.25 + ☐ = £8.00

4. Put these decimals in ascending order (ascending means smallest to largest):

9.7   5.6   0.45   0.02   3.09   2.4

Activity

Look back at the Number Square you did on page 4.
Seeing decimal numbers laid out like this can help you
work out how to add them or order them.

Check Your Progress!

Decimals ☐

Turn to page 48 and put a tick next to what you have just learned.

Parents Start Here...

Practising addition is the best way for your child to revise. Children are allowed to use calculators in one of their two maths papers so encourage them to check their answers with a calculator.

Practise Adding

Remember!

- You can use whatever methods you prefer to add.
- Try to use mental methods whenever you can.
- Estimate an answer first and you will avoid making silly mistakes.
- Check your answer afterwards.

1. These pyramids are made from number cards. Add two numbers on the bottom row and put the answer in the box above. Complete each pyramid to find the number at the top:

a)

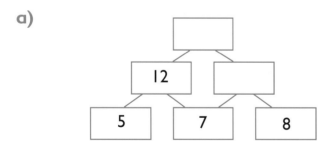

b)

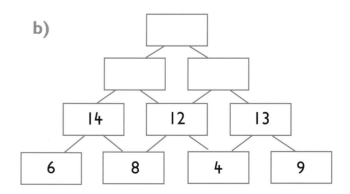

c)

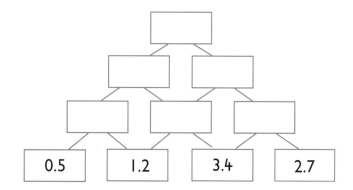

| 0.5 | 1.2 | 3.4 | 2.7 |

d) What would happen if you shuffled the cards on the bottom row around? Would you get the same total at the top? Try it and see.

2. Add four numbers in a straight line. Do this as many ways as you can. The lines can be vertical, horizontal or diagonal.

Write the numbers around the edge of the grid.

4	5	0	6
2	9	3	8
4	6	5	7
4	6	8	5

a) What is the smallest total you can make? _____

b) What is the largest total you can make? _____

Activity

Create your own grids and pyramids like the ones you have completed here. Try doing some with decimals too.

Check Your Progress!
Practise Adding
Turn to page 48 and put a tick next to what you have just learned.

Top Tip! If your child struggles with anything, don't worry – let them go at their own pace.

Parents Start Here...

Children should be able to answer most of these questions using mental maths strategies, or simple jottings on paper. If your child finds this difficult, then they need more practice to prepare for their SATs.

Subtraction

Remember!

- Subtraction is the inverse (opposite) of addition.

- Knowing number bonds helps you subtract in your head.

- Remember to bounce backwards when you subtract on a number line.

- You can use whatever method you like to subtract but show your working if you have not done the calculation in your head.

1. a) The difference between 75 and 100 is ☐

   b) The difference between 44 and 100 is ☐

   c) The difference between 36 and 90 is ☐

   d) The difference between 16 and 50 is ☐

2. Join the pairs of numbers that make 100:

   35   15   54   80   70   65   20   30   46   85

3. Join the pairs of numbers that make 1000:

99   450   200   427   573   901   550   800

4. Join the pairs of numbers that make 76:

52   12   24   64   35   80   41   -4

5. Write numbers in the boxes to make this correct:

17 + ⬜ − ⬜ = 17

6. Margie had £5.00 and gave Matt £3.46. How much money did she have left?

Activity

Start at any number between 100 and 1000 and try to count backwards in groups of 10. If this is too easy try to count back in groups of 9.

Check Your Progress!

Subtraction ⬜

Turn to page 48 and put a tick next to what you have just learned.

Parents Start Here...

Remind your child that in a number like 831 the 3 represents 30 not 3 units. This helps them to avoid getting confused when subtracting on paper.

Working Subtractions Out On Paper

Remember!

- You can subtract on paper using a column method, chopping numbers up (partitioning) or by repeated additions.

- Use whichever method you prefer, but make sure you can do it correctly.

- Practice makes perfect – it really does get easier the more often you do it.

1. Partitioning

Look at this subtraction and then complete the others. Remember to chop the numbers up into easier chunks.

$$45 - 33 = ?$$
$$40 - 30 = 10$$
$$5 - 3 = 2$$
$$10 + 2 = 12$$

The answer is 12

a) 97 – 45 = ☐

b) 56 – 13 = ☐

c) 87 – 26 = ☐

2. Repeated Addition

Look at this subtraction and then complete the others. Remember you just keep adding chunks to the smaller number until you get to the big number.

```
    253
  – 145
  ─────
  +  55  ←──You need 55 more to make 200.
  ─────
    200
  ─────
  +  53  ←──Then 53 more to get to 253.
  ─────
    253      55 + 53 = 108 ←── So you have to add on 55 + 53 to get from 145 to 253 = 108.
```

a)   657
     – 458
     ───────

b)   396
     – 278
     ───────

c)   703
     – 555
     ───────

3. Column Method

Look at this subtraction and then complete the others.

```
   5 1
   5̶6̶7
  – 238
  ─────
    329
```

a)   764
     – 549
     ───────

b)   574
     – 293
     ───────

c)   831
     – 248
     ───────

Activity

Your parents probably did not learn to subtract using all these methods; see if you can teach them how to do it!

Check Your Progress!
Working Subtractions Out On Paper ☐

Turn to page 48 and put a tick next to what you have just learned.

Top Tip!
Go through any of the questions on these pages as often as you like until your child understands it fully.

Parents Start Here...

When children encounter problem-solving questions they are expected to break down the question into simpler steps and identify the information they need to carry out the tasks.

Practise Subtracting

Remember!

- Estimate your answers before you begin each one.

- Remember that it matters where you put the decimal point.

- Check your answers with a calculator afterwards.

- Remember – if you know what 8 x 4 is, then 4 x 8 is the same.

1. You pay for each item on the chart with a £10 note. Write in the change you get each time:

Item	Number of items you buy	Cost for each item	Change from £10
a) School Bag	1	£6.99	
b) Handwriting Pens	3	75p	
c) Trading Cards	2	£1.48	
d) Gym Shoes	1	£2.99	
e) Tracksuit	1	£8.50	

How much money did you spend altogether? _____

2. Tom was thinking of a two digit number less than 50. The sum of the two digits was 12. The difference between the two digits was 4. What was the number Tom was thinking of?

_____

3. A tree grows 30 cm every year. The farmer kept a record of its height every year, but then he lost the piece of paper. He knows how tall it is now. Help the farmer write out his record again:

Year	Height
2004	297 cm
a) 2003	☐
b) 2002	☐
c) 2001	☐

d) How tall was the tree in 1997? ☐

Activity

TRY THIS

Ask someone to think of a number less than 100. You have 20 questions to find out what it is but the other person can only answer "yes" or "no". Try asking questions like "is it even?" or "is it more than 50?".

Check Your Progress!
Practise Subtracting ☐
Turn to page 48 and put a tick next to what you have just learned.

Top Tip!
Remember to give your child lots of praise – they will work so much better.

Parents Start Here...

Much of modern mathematics requires children to perform mental calculations. This can be a laborious and difficult task for a child who does not know their tables.

Times Tables

Remember!

- You must know all of your Times Tables up to 10.

- If you know your Times Tables challenge yourself to learn tables to 20.

1. Time yourself as you answer the questions on this page. When you have finished the page put a piece of paper over your answers and do them all over again. See if you can get them all right in less time. Give yourself a 10 second penalty for every answer you get wrong.

5 x 7 = ☐   3 x 4 = ☐

9 x 9 = ☐   8 x 10 = ☐

5 x 5 = ☐   9 x 6 = ☐

6 x 10 = ☐   7 x 7 = ☐

8 x 2 = ☐   4 x 9 = ☐

9 x 4 = ☐   6 x 6 = ☐

10 x 2 = ☐   6 x 6 = ☐

3 x 6 = ☐   4 x 4 = ☐

5 x 7 = ☐   3 x 9 = ☐

4 x 8 = ☐   3 x 5 = ☐

9 x 9 = ☐   5 x 7 = ☐

2 x 6 = ☐   7 x 9 = ☐

6 x 7 = ☐   9 x 2 = ☐

7 x 8 = ☐   3 x 3 = ☐

8 x 9 = ☐   8 x 6 = ☐

7 x 2 = ☐   8 x 8 = ☐

Ask an adult to mark your answers for you.

Activity

Draw your own multiplication table with all the numbers from 1 to 10 along the top and down the side. You need 11 rows along the top and 11 columns down. Fill it in as quickly as you can.

Check Your Progress!
Times Tables ☐

Turn to page 48 and put a tick next to what you have just learned.

21

Parents Start Here...

Top Tip! Try and incorporate what your child learns into everyday life – they will remember it even better.

Children are expected to multiply two digit numbers by a single digit number in their heads (e.g. 56 x 9). They learn different strategies to help them do this.

Multiplication

Remember!

- When you multiply two numbers the answer is called the product.

- Before you can multiply numbers you need to know what each digit means.

- You can chop numbers up – or partition them – to make multiplying easier.

1. Chop these numbers up. The first one has been done for you:

   a) 457   =   400 + 50 + 7

   b) 569   =   _____

   c) 6792 =   _____

   d) 732   =   _____

   e) 470   =   _____

2. You can use your tables to work out harder multiplications in your head:

   11 x 8 = 10 x 8 plus one more 8 = 88

Use your tables to complete these multiplications in your head:

a) 15 x 7 = _____

(hint: try 10 x 7, then 5 x 7 and add the products together)

b) 15 x 9 = _____

c) 20 x 3 = _____

d) 20 x 6 = _____

e) 14 x 3 = _____

(hint: try 7 x 3 then double the answer)

f) 16 x 4 = _____

g) 40 x 8 = _____

h) 19 x 6 = _____

(hint: work out 20 x 6 then take 6 away)

i) 21 x 6 = _____

3. Josephine needs to buy 66 duvets for her hotel and each one costs £5.
Can you work out how much the duvets will cost her?

Activity

The next time you are on a long and boring car journey
try multiplying all the digits in a car number plate (e.g. 4 x
5 x 6). Then try multiplying them as two digit numbers
(e.g. 45 x 6 and 4 x 56). The winner is the person who can
make the largest number.

Check Your Progress!
Multiplication

Turn to page 48 and put a tick next to what you have just learned.

Top Tip!
If your child loses concentration here, let them take a break.

Parents Start Here...

Adding a zero to multiply by 10 works well with whole numbers, but gets confusing when you are multiplying numbers less than 1 (e.g. 0.34) so it is best to encourage your child to move the digits to the left.

Multiplying By 10, 100 And 1000

Remember!

- You can multiply by 10, 100 or 1000 in your head.

- You can add zeros to get the answers but the best way is to imagine you are moving all the digits to the left:

  $56 \times 10 = 560$
  $56 \times 100 = 5600$
  $56 \times 1000 = 56\ 000$

- You can multiply by 20 if you multiply by 10 then double the answer.

1. Write in the missing numbers:

a) $34 \times \boxed{} = 340$

b) $34 \times \boxed{} = 3400$

c) $3.4 \times \boxed{} = 34$

d) $0.34 \times \boxed{} = 34$

e) $3400 \times \boxed{} = 34\ 000$

f) $0.034 \times \boxed{} = 34$

Now check all of your answers with a calculator.

2. Tick the correct answer:

a) 46.3 x 10 =

463 ☐

4.63 ☐

4630 ☐

b) 934 x 100 =

93.4 ☐

9340 ☐

93 400 ☐

c) 20 x 71 =

1420 ☐

710 ☐

142 ☐

d) 0.8 x 10 =

80 ☐

8 ☐

0.08 ☐

e) 1009 x 20 =

10 090 ☐

20 180 ☐

2018 ☐

Activity

We find it easy to do mental maths when the numbers are 10s, 100s and 1000s. Why do you think this is?

Check Your Progress!
Multiplying By 10, 100 And 1000 ☐
Turn to page 48 and put a tick next to what you have just learned.

25

Parents Start Here...

Number patterns and sequences are covered in Key Stage One. At Key Stage Two children can use these patterns to predict answers and discover relationships between numbers.

Multiples

Remember!

- When you count in 10s we say you are counting in multiples of 10.

- 10, 20, 30, etc, all are multiples of 10.

- You can work out the multiples for any number.

1. Complete the number sequences:

a) 55, 60, 65, ☐, ☐, ☐   These are all multiples of ☐

b) 72, 74, ☐, ☐, ☐, ☐   These are all multiples of ☐

c) 800, 700, ☐, ☐, ☐, ☐   These are all multiples of ☐

2. Circle the number that is not a multiple:

a) Multiples of 4:

16   40   24   26   36   48

b) Multiples of 9:

81   63   53   45   18   90

c) Multiples of 11:

33   66   78   88   22   99

d) Multiples of 15:

45   90   95   30   75   60

3. Write 3 multiples of both 2 and 5: _____   _____   _____

4. Write 3 multiples of both 4 and 6: _____   _____   _____

5. Write 3 multiples of both 3 and 11: _____   _____   _____

6. Write 3 multiples of both 25 and 10: _____   _____   _____

7. Frank was thinking about a multiple of 6. When he doubled it he got 72. What was the number Frank was thinking of?

_____

Activity

Counting in multiples is fast; try to count in multiples of 50 and see how far you can get.

Check Your Progress!

Multiples ☐

Turn to page 48 and put a tick next to what you have just learned.

Top Tip!
If your child struggles with anything, don't worry – let them go at their own pace.

Parents Start Here...

Using the grid method helps children really understand the numbers they are working with. Remind them that the digit 1 in 415 represents 10, not 1.

Multiplying On Paper: The Grid Method

Remember!

- When you multiply two numbers the answer is called the product.

- Estimate your answer before you begin to avoid silly mistakes.

- You can chop the numbers up using the Grid Method of Multiplication.

Look at this multiplication:

$$134 \times 37 =$$

You can chop the numbers up and put them in a grid.
Add up all of your totals to get the final answer.

x	100	30	4	Totals
30	3000	900 add →	120	4020
7	700	210 add →	28	938
				4958

add ↓

The product is 4958.

Use the grid method to answer these problems:

a) **703 x 23 =**

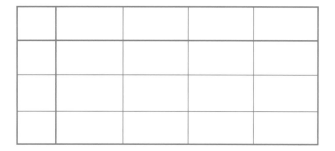

b) **415 x 56 =**

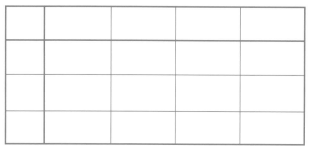

c) **68 x 91 =**

d) **402 x 18 =**

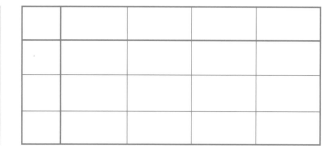

Check your answers with a calculator.

Activity

Teach your Mum or Dad how to do partitioning and multiplying like this. Adults were not usually taught this method so you will be doing them a favour. When you teach someone a topic it helps you revise it too.

Check Your Progress!
   Multiplying On Paper: The Grid Method
Turn to page 48 and put a tick next to what you have just learned.

Top Tip!
Learning is fun, so if your child is tired, let them come back to this when they are fresh.

Parents Start Here...

This is probably the method you are more familiar with. Encourage your child to estimate the answers before they begin. They can do this by rounding the numbers up or down.

Multiplying Using The Column Method

Remember!

- When you are confident of the Grid Method of multiplying you can practise the Column Method.

- The Column Method is quick and takes up much less room – but it is easier to make mistakes.

- You must show your working.

- Keep all of your digits in the correct column and ensure your writing is very neat. If you can't keep your numbers in line try using squared paper.

Look at this multiplication:

$27 \times 16 =$

Step One:		**t**	**u**	
		2	7	$7 \times 6 = 42$
	$\times$	1	₄6	put the units in the units column
			2	carry over the 4

Step Two:				
		2	7	$6 \times 2 = 12$
	$\times$	1	₄6	$12 + 4 = 16$
	1	6	2	put the answer here

Step Three: Remember to put a zero in the units column.

```
          2   7
     x    1   6
          1   6   2      put a zero in the units column
          2   7   0
```

1 x 2 = 2
put the answer here 2 7

1 x 7 = 7   put the answer here

Step Four: Add the totals together.

```
          2   7
     x    1   6
          1   6   2      put a zero in the units column
   +      2   7   0
          4   3   2
          1
```

Use the Column Method to complete these multiplications:
You may need to use a separate piece of paper for your working out.

a) 55 x 27 =
b) 128 x 12 =
c) 93 x 56 =
d) 44 x 66 =

Check your answers with a calculator. If you got any wrong try the calculations again using the Grid Method to help you find out where you went wrong.

Activity

Put some big numbers into your calculator and try multiplying them by 0.5. What happens to the numbers?

Check Your Progress!
   Multiplying Using The Column Method
Turn to page 48 and put a tick next to what you have just learned.

Top Tip!
Remember to give your child lots of praise – they will work so much better.

Parents Start Here...

It does not matter how your child works out the square numbers in Question 4, as long as they do not use a calculator. You can remind them of some of the methods they have already looked at.

Square Numbers And Square Roots

Remember!

- When a number is multiplied by itself the product is a square number.

- We show a number is squared like this: $5^2 = 25$.

- The number that is multiplied by itself is called a square root.

1. a) How many small squares are in the top row of this square? _____5_____

b) How many small squares are down the first column of the square? _____5_____

c) Count all of the small squares and write the total here: _____25_____

d) Explain how square numbers get their name:

They got their name

_____

_____

2. Join the square number up to its square root. One has been done for you:

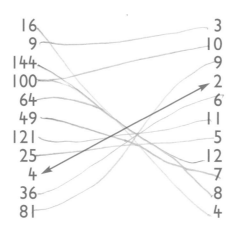

3. Complete the multiplications as quickly as you can:

a) $6 \times 6 = 6^2 = \boxed{36}$ **b)** $11 \times 11 = \boxed{11^2} = \boxed{121}$ **c)** $8 \times 8 = \boxed{8^2} = \boxed{64}$

d) $9 \times 9 = \boxed{9^2} = \boxed{81}$ **e)** $7 \times 7 = \boxed{7^2} = \boxed{49}$

4.

$12^2 = \boxed{144}$

$13^2 = \boxed{169}$

$14^2 = \boxed{196}$

$15^2 = \boxed{225}$

$16^2 = 256$

the difference between these numbers is $\boxed{25}$

the difference between these numbers is $\boxed{27}$

the difference between these numbers is $\boxed{29}$

31

Look at the number pattern. Now you can say what 16^2 is very easily: $16^2 = \boxed{256}$

Activity

Find the square root button on your calculator. It looks like this: $\sqrt{\ }$. Practise finding the square roots of big numbers. Most of them will be decimals, but see if you can get some whole numbers.

Check Your Progress!
Square Numbers And Square Roots ☐
Turn to page 48 and put a tick next to what you have just learned.

Top Tip!
Go through any of the questions on these pages as often as you like until your child understands it fully.

Parents Start Here...

Doubling and halving are taught in Key Stage One and Key Stage Two. They are very useful mental maths strategies. Teachers will often quick-fire doubling and halving questions at their students during mental maths sessions.

Doubling And Halving

Remember!

- When you multiply a number by 2 you are doubling it.

- When you divide a number by 2 you are halving it.

- Halving and doubling numbers can help you solve mathematical problems.

- Sometimes it is easier to round a number up or down before you halve or double it.

1. Chopping the numbers up can help to double or halve them,
   e.g. to double 54: double 50 and double 4 then add the totals:

$$50 + 50 = 100$$
$$4 + 4 = 8$$
$$100 + 8 = 108$$

Use this method to match the numbers to their doubles. One has been done for you:

a) 73	104
b) 92	166
c) 76	4048
d) 2024	152
e) 2110	184
f) 83	4220
g) 52	146

2. Round numbers up or down before you double them:
   e.g. To double 59, double 60 first then take away 2:

$$60 + 60 = 120$$
$$120 - 2 = 118$$

Use this method to double these numbers. Try to do them in your head:

a) 79 _____

b) 68 _____

c) 49 _____

3. a) Mrs Mooch has 7.5 metres of fabric to cover her armchairs. She has two armchairs that are the same size. How much fabric will she have for each one?

_____

b) Eddie the Emu is looking after the eggs while Ellie is out. Unfortunately he has lost half of them. He started off with 114 eggs. How many are left?

_____

c) Jack says to Jill "I am thinking of a number. Now I have halved it and halved it again. The number I am left with is 16. What number was I thinking of?"
Jill quickly works out Jack's original number. "That's easy," she says, "when you know that doubling is the opposite of halving."

What was Jack's original number? _____

Activity

Think up a problem like the one Jack set Jill. Include as much doubling and halving as you can.

If you have a dartboard look at the 'doubles' – how much is each one worth? With darts you can quickly learn all the doubles up to 20. There are also trebles. Can you work out what each of them is worth?

Check Your Progress!
Doubling And Halving
Turn to page 48 and put a tick next to what you have just learned.

Parents Start Here...

Is your child comfortable with mathematical vocabulary? It is important that they know what mathematical terms mean and how to use them appropriately.

Factors And Prime Numbers

Remember!

- Factors are numbers that divide into other numbers without any remainders.

- The factors of 10 are 1, 2, 5, and 10.

- Prime numbers are numbers that can not be divided by any number except 1 and themselves.

- 1 is not a prime number.

- 2 is the only prime number that ends in a 2.

- Apart from 2 and 5 all prime numbers end in 1, 3, 7 or 9.

1. a) Write all the factors of 12: _____

   b) Write all the factors of 24: _____

   c) Write all the factors of 48: _____

2. All of our coins are factors of what number?
Tick the correct answer:

   a) £1.00 ☐

   b) 50p ☐

c) £2.00 ☐

d) £3.00 ☐

3. This number square goes up to 100. Circle all of the prime numbers you can find:

1	2	3	4	5	6	7	8	9	10
11	12	13	14	15	16	17	18	19	20
21	22	23	24	25	26	27	28	29	30
31	32	33	34	35	36	37	38	39	40
41	42	43	44	45	46	47	48	49	50
51	52	53	54	55	56	57	58	59	60
61	62	63	64	65	66	67	68	69	70
71	72	73	74	75	76	77	78	79	80
81	82	83	84	85	86	87	88	89	90
91	92	93	94	95	96	97	98	99	100

Activity

To help you check if you have all the factors remember that they come in pairs (if you multiply the pair together, you get the large number) e.g. for 20 the pairs are 1 and 20, 2 and 10, 4 and 5. Use this method to check you have all the factors for Question 1 and for any factor questions you try in the future.

Check Your Progress!
Factors And Prime Numbers ☐
Turn to page 48 and put a tick next to what you have just learned.

Parents Start Here...

It is best to take the subject of division slowly. Children learn the basics in Key Stage Two but many find it a difficult topic. If your child is struggling revert back to the 'sharing out' idea and use buttons or coins to show what a division means.

Division

Remember!

- Division means sharing out.

- You might also say 'how many times does x goes into y'.

- Dividing is the inverse (opposite) of multiplying.

- There are different ways of doing division; use the method you are happiest with.

1. Dividing by 10 or 100:
When you divide by 10 or 100 you can move the digits to the right.

$625 \div 10 = 62.5$
$625 \div 100 = 6.25$

If in doubt, round the numbers up or down to get a rough estimate first:
$600 \div 10 = 60$

a) $772 \div 100 =$ _____

b) $902 \div 10 =$ _____

c) $43 \div 100 =$ _____

d) $67 \div 10 =$ _____

2. Dividing by 20 or 200:

Divide by 10 or 100 first then halve the answer:

a) $46 \div 20 =$ _____

b) $88 \div 20 =$ _____

c) $160 \div 20 =$ _____

d) $2066 \div 200 =$ _____

e) $4228 \div 200 =$ _____

3. Use your knowledge of tables to do these divisions:

a) I had 15 apples which I shared between 3 friends. They got ☐ apples each.

b) Bill had 72 doughnuts to give to 8 hungry camels. They got ☐ doughnuts each.

c) Clara and Peter had 56 goats. There were 8 goats in each pen. Clara and Peter had ☐ pens altogether.

4. Some divisions have a number left over. This is called a remainder.

a) $75 \div 7 =$ ☐ remainder: ☐

b) $82 \div 9 =$ ☐ remainder: ☐

c) $146 \div 12 =$ ☐ remainder: ☐

d) $16 \div 5 =$ ☐ remainder: ☐

TRY THIS

Activity

Look back at your divisions with remainders. Can you use the remainders to round up or down to the nearest ten?

Check Your Progress!

Division ☐

Turn to page 48 and put a tick next to what you have just learned.

Top Tip! If your child loses concentration here, let them take a break.

Parents Start Here...

You may not be familiar with this method but it is a successful way to teach children division because it can be set at a very simple level to begin with, then gradually made more complex. Children find they can do the calculations in fewer steps as they progress.

Dividing By Repeated Subtraction

Remember!

- One way to work out divisions on paper is to break the big number into chunks that you can divide more easily. This is called repeated subtraction.

- Make a sensible estimate of the answer before you begin; you can do this by rounding.

- You must write down all your working.

- Check your answer makes sense.

1. **567 ÷ 45 = ?**

   You know that 45 will go into the big number at least 10 times, because 10 x 45 = 450. You can then take this chunk off the big number and see how many times 45 goes into the number that is left.

$$
\begin{array}{r}
45\overline{)567} \\
-\quad 450 \\
\hline
117 \\
-\quad 90 \\
\hline
27
\end{array}
$$

(x 10) 45 goes into 567 **10** times

(x 2) 45 goes into 90 **2** times

add these numbers (10 + 2)

45 goes into 567
12 times with a remainder of 27

Use this method of repeated subtraction to answer the following questions:

a) 860 ÷ 85 =

b) 742 ÷ 71 =

c) 87 ÷ 15 =

d) 145 ÷ 13 =

e) 119 ÷ 8 =

Activity

Using a calculator to check your division answers is not straightforward if you have a remainder because calculators turn remainders into fractions. There is a way to do it, though. Experiment and see if you can find it.

Check Your Progress!
Dividing By Repeated Subtraction
Turn to page 48 and put a tick next to what you have just learned.

Top Tip!
If your child struggles with anything, don't worry – let them go at their own pace.

Parents Start Here...

Long and short divisions are probably the terms you remember from school. Not all children learn these methods at Key Stage Two because not everyone is ready for it by the end of Year Six.

Short And Long Division

Remember!

- You can also divide by 'carrying over'. It does not take up so much room on the page but it is easier to make silly mistakes.

- Estimate a sensible answer first.

- Keep your writing neat and put all the digits in the correct column.

- Check your answer afterwards.

Note: If you have not learnt this method at school then you can leave these pages and go straight on to pages 44–45.

I. Short Division

With this method you carry over any remainders to the next column. Start on the left and work towards the units:

Short division

$$695 \div 2 = \quad 2\overline{)69^15} \quad \overset{347 r1}{}$$

2 goes into 9 4 times with remainder 1.

Carry the remainder over to the next column.

Use short division to work out this problem:

The Headteacher at St Ann's School had 462 lemon sherbets to share out between Form 1, Form 2 and Form 3. How many lemon sherbets did she give each form? Use a separate piece of paper.

2. Long Division

With this method you write any remainders below and bring the next number down to join it. Start on the left and work towards the units:

Long division

$$439 \div 3 = \quad 3\overline{)439}^{146}$$

$$\begin{array}{r} 146 \\ 3\overline{)439} \\ \underline{3} \\ 13 \\ \underline{-12} \\ 19 \\ \underline{-18} \\ r\ 1 \end{array}$$

Use long division to work out this problem:

Farmer Milo had 541 potatoes to plant in 4 rows. How many potatoes went into each row, and how many were left over? Use a separate piece of paper.

Activity

Play this game. It has nothing to do with dividing. Ask another player to write down two numbers less than ten. You have to work out the numbers, with two clues: the sum of the two numbers and their product.

Check Your Progress!
Short And Long Division

Turn to page 48 and put a tick next to what you have just learned.

Parents Start Here...

The use of brackets is included the Key Stage Two Maths curriculum; children are expected to understand that brackets show them what order to do things in.

Calculating With Brackets

Remember!

- **Brackets** are used in calculations to show what should be done first.

- **Brackets** help to stop confusion in more complicated problems.

- There must be an opening bracket (and a closing bracket) every time.

For example:

$$5 \times 6 + 3 = 33$$
$$5 \times (6 + 3) = 45$$

The digits and the symbols are all the same, but the brackets make a big difference to the answer.

1. a) $(3 + 8) \times (8 - 4) =$ _____

   b) $(9 + 2) \times (10 - 7) =$ _____

   c) $(4 + 8) \div (15 \div 5) =$ _____

   d) $(75 \times 2) - (5 \times 25) =$ _____

   e) $(3.4 \times 10) + (0.2 \times 100) =$ _____

   f) $(0.1 + 0.9) - (0.5 + 0.5) =$ _____

2. The sign **>** means **MORE THAN**   10 > 9 means 10 is **MORE THAN** 9

The sign **<** means less than   0.3 < 3 means 0.3 is less than 3

Put the correct sign in:

e.g. (10 + 2) > (11 – 3)

a) (14 × 2) ☐ (5 × 5)   b) (70 ÷ 2) ☐ (7 × 6)

c) (9 × 9) ☐ (8 × 8)   d) (45 ÷ 9) ☐ (35 ÷ 5)

e) (20 ÷ 2) ☐ (13 – 5)   f) (11 × 3) ☐ (6 × 6)

g) (16 + 4) ☐ (7 × 3)   h) (5 × 7) ☐ (64 ÷ 2)

Activity

Your calculator may not have brackets, but it does have a memory function. You can use the memory button to help you work out problems with brackets. Not all calculators work the same way so you either need to read the instructions or experiment...

Check Your Progress!
Calculating With Brackets   ☐
Turn to page 48 and put a tick next to what you have just learned.

Answers

Pages 4–5

1.

0.1	0.2	0.3	0.4	0.5	0.6	0.7	0.8	0.9	1
1.1	1.2	1.3	1.4	1.5	1.6	1.7	1.8	1.9	2
2.1	2.2	2.3	2.4	2.5	2.6	2.7	2.8	2.9	3
3.1	3.2	3.3	3.4	3.5	3.6	3.7	3.8	3.9	4
4.1	4.2	4.3	4.4	4.5	4.6	4.7	4.8	4.9	5
5.1	5.2	5.3	5.4	5.5	5.6	5.7	5.8	5.9	6
6.1	6.2	6.3	6.4	6.5	6.6	6.7	6.8	6.9	7
7.1	7.2	7.3	7.4	7.5	7.6	7.7	7.8	7.9	8
8.1	8.2	8.3	8.4	8.5	8.6	8.7	8.8	8.9	9
9.1	9.2	9.3	9.4	9.5	9.6	9.7	9.8	9.9	10

2. a) Three hundred and forty
b) One thousand five hundred and two
c) Ninety eight

3.

	100s	10s	units	10ths	100ths
346.3	300	40	6	3	0
45.03		40	5	0	3
0.98				9	8
904.56	900	0	4	5	6
70.24		70	0	2	4

4. a) 80 000
b) 4 hundredths, or 0.04
c) 6323

Pages 6–7

1. a) 96
b) 63
c) 89
d) 98
2. a) 81
b) 69
c) 100
d) 98
3. a) 64
b) 64
c) 55
d) 55
4. 56

Pages 8–9

1. a) 1
b) -1
c) -12
d) -7
e) -59
f) -84
g) -11

Pages 10–11

1. b) 8.8 → 9
c) 2.4 → 2
d) 45.5 → 46
2. a) 7
b) 60
c) £3.00
d) £79.00
3. a) 0.9
b) 0.7
c) £0.75 (or 75p)
4. 0.02, 0.45, 2.4, 3.09, 5.6, 9.7

Pages 12–13

1. a) 27
b) 51
c) 17
d) The number would change because the numbers in the middle get added more often than the numbers on the edges.
2. a) 14
b) 26

Pages 14–15

1. a) 25
b) 56
c) 54
d) 34
2. 35 + 65
15 + 85
54 + 46
80 + 20
70 + 30
3. 99 + 901
450 + 550
200 + 800
427 + 573
4. 52 + 24
12 + 64
35 + 41
80 + -4
5. 17 + 17 − 17 = 17
6. £1.54

Pages 16–17

1. a) 52
b) 43
c) 61
2. a) 199
b) 118
c) 148
4. a) 215
b) 281
c) 583

Pages 18–19

1. a) £3.01
b) £7.75
c) £7.04
d) £7.01
e) £1.50
The total cost was £23.69.
2. 48
3. a) 267 cm
b) 237 cm
c) 207 cm
3. 87 cm

Pages 20–21

You can check your answers against the Multiplication Table you have completed.

Pages 22–23

1. b) 500 + 60 + 9
c) 6000 + 700 + 90 + 2
d) 700 + 30 + 2
e) 400 + 70
2. a) 105
b) 135

c) 60
d) 120
e) 42
f) 64
g) 320
h) 114
i) 126
3. £330

Pages 24–25

1. a) 10
b) 100
c) 10
d) 100
e) 10
f) 1000
2. a) 463
b) 93 400
c) 1420
d) 8
e) 20 180

Pages 26–27

1. a) 70, 75, 80 = multiples of 5
b) 76, 78, 80, 82 = multiples of 2
c) 600, 500, 400, 300 = multiples of 100
2. a) 26
b) 53
c) 78
d) 95
3. 10, 20, 30, etc.
4. 12, 24, 48, 60, etc.
5. 33, 66, 99, etc.
6. 100, 150, 200, 250, etc.
7. 36

Pages 28–29

a) 16 169
b) 23 240
c) 6188
d) 7236

Pages 30–31

a) 1485
b) 1536
c) 5208
d) 2904

Pages 32–33

1. a) 5
b) 5
c) 25
d) When you multiply one number by itself, and put the numbers into a grid, a square is created.
2. $9 \rightarrow 3$
$16 \rightarrow 4$
$25 \rightarrow 5$
$36 \rightarrow 6$
$49 \rightarrow 7$
$64 \rightarrow 8$
$81 \rightarrow 9$
$100 \rightarrow 10$
$121 \rightarrow 11$
$144 \rightarrow 12$
3. a) 36
b) $11^2, 121$
c) $8^2, 64$
d) $9^2, 81$
e) $7^2, 49$
4.

$16^2 = 256$

Pages 34–35

1. a) 146
b) 184
c) 152
d) 4048
e) 4220
f) 166
2. a) 158
b) 136
c) 98
3. a) 3.75 metres
b) 57
c) 64

Pages 36–37

1. a) 1, 2, 3, 4, 6, 12
b) 1, 2, 3, 4, 6, 8, 12, 24

c) 1, 2, 3, 4, 6, 8, 12, 24, 48
2. c
3. 2, 5, 11, 13, 17, 19, 23, 31, 33, 37, 41, 43, 47, 51, 53, 57, 59, 61, 67, 73, 77, 79, 83, 87, 89, 91, 97

Pages 38–39

1. a) 7.72
b) 90.2
c) 0.43
d) 6.7
2. a) 2.3
b) 4.4
c) 8
d) 10.33
e) 21.14
3. a) 5
b) 9
c) 7
4. a) 10 remainder 5
b) 9 remainder 1
c) 12 remainder 2
d) 3 remainder 1

Pages 40–41

1. a) 10 remainder 10
b) 10 remainder 32
c) 5 remainder 12
d) 11 remainder 2
e) 14 remainder 7

Pages 42–43

1. a) 154
b) 135 potatoes went into each row, with 1 left over.

Pages 44–45

1. a) 44
b) 33
c) 4
d) 25
e) 54
f) 0
2. a) 28 > 25   b) 35 < 42
c) 81 > 64   d) 5 < 7
e) 10 > 8   f) 33 < 36
g) 20 < 21   h) 35 > 32

Check Your Progress!

Ordering Numbers . . . . □

Adding Up To 100 . . . . □

Negative Numbers . . . . □

Decimals . . . . □

Practise Adding . . . . □

Subtraction . . . . □

Working Subtractions Out On Paper . . . . □

Practise Subtracting . . . . □

Times Tables . . . . □

Multiplication . . . . □

Multiplying By 10, 100 And 1000 . . . . □

Multiples . . . . □

Multiplying On Paper: The Grid Method . . . . □

Multiplying Using The Column Method . . . . □

Square Numbers And Square Roots . . . . □

Doubling And Halving . . . . □

Factors And Prime Numbers . . . . □

Division . . . . □

Dividing By Repeated Subtraction . . . . □

Short And Long Division . . . . □

Calculating With Brackets . . . . □